Teaching Vocabulary
to Improve
Reading Comprehension

Teaching Vocabulary to Improve Reading Comprehension

William E. Nagy
Center for the Study of Reading
University of Illinois at Urbana-Champaign

ERIC Clearinghouse on Reading and
Communication Skills

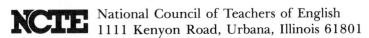 National Council of Teachers of English
1111 Kenyon Road, Urbana, Illinois 61801

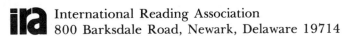 International Reading Association
800 Barksdale Road, Newark, Delaware 19714

IRA Publications Committee, 1988–89: Robert L. Schreiner, *Chair*; Phyllis E. Brazee; Kent L. Brown, Jr.; Margaret K. Jensen; Charles K. Kinzer; Gloria M. McDonell; Allan R. Neilsen; Tom Nicholson; Donna Ogle; John J. Pikulski; Anne C. Tarleton; Ronald W. Mitchell, *Executive Director;* Jennifer A. Stevenson, *Director of Publications*

Book Design: Interior, Tom Kovacs for TGK Design; cover, Michael J. Getz

NCTE Stock Number 52384

Published 1988 by the ERIC Clearinghouse on Reading and Communication Skills, the National Council of Teachers of English, and the International Reading Association. Printed in the United States of America.

This publication was prepared with funding from the Office of Educational Research and Improvement, U.S. Department of Education, under contract no. 400-86-0045. Contractors undertaking such projects under government sponsorship are encouraged to express freely their judgment in professional and technical matters. Prior to publication, the manuscript was submitted to the Editorial Board of the National Council of Teachers of English and the Publications Committee of the International Reading Association for critical review and determination of professional competence. This publication has met such standards. Points of view or opinions, however, do not necessarily represent the official view or opinions of the National Council of Teachers of English, the International Reading Association, or the Office of Educational Research and Improvement.

Library of Congress Cataloging-in-Publication Data
Nagy, William E.
    Teaching vocabulary to improve reading comprehension / William E. Nagy.
        p. cm.
    Bibliography: p.
    ISBN 0-8141-5238-4. ISBN 0-87207-151-0 (International Reading Association)
        1. Vocabulary — Study and teaching (Elementary) — United States. 2. Reading comprehension — Study and teaching (Elementary) — United States. I. Title.
LB1574.5.N34 1988
372.4'144 — dc19   88-24618
                                                                        CIP

Eleventh Printing, July 2000

Contents

Acknowledgments

I want to express my gratitude to Janice Dole and Patricia Herman, my colleagues at the Center for the Study of Reading; our many discussions helped me immeasurably in gaining a better understanding of practical issues in vocabulary instruction. I also wish to thank Charles Suhor for suggesting the inclusion of numerous specific activities and illustrations. With this help from my friends, I hope that I have been able to help bridge the gap between research and classroom application.

William Nagy

Grateful acknowledgment is also made to the *Illinois English Bulletin* for permission to reprint "The AIM Game," by Charles Suhor (*IEB* 70, no. 3: 1–3).

Foreword

This book was developed during the period when the ERIC Clearinghouse on Reading and Communication Skills (ERIC/RCS) was sponsored by the National Council of Teachers of English. The Educational Resources Information Center (ERIC) is a national information system developed by the U.S. Department of Education and sponsored by the Office of Educational Research and Improvement (OERI). ERIC provides ready access to descriptions of exemplary programs, research and development reports, and related information useful in developing effective educational programs.

Through its network of specialized centers, or clearinghouses, each of which is responsible for a particular educational area, ERIC acquires, evaluates, abstracts, and indexes current significant information and lists this information in its reference publications.

The ERIC system has already made available — through the ERIC Document Reproduction Service — a considerable body of data, including all federally funded research reports since 1956. However, if the findings of educational research are to be used by teachers, much of the data must be translated into an essentially different context. Rather than resting at the point of making research reports readily accessible, OERI has directed the ERIC clearinghouses to commission authorities in various fields to write information analysis papers.

This book, then, is the most recent practitioner-oriented text developed by ERIC/RCS in cooperation with the National Council of Teachers of English and the International Reading Association. The Clearinghouse, NCTE, and IRA hope that the materials are helpful in clarifying important educational issues and in improving classroom practice.

Karl Koenke
Associate Director, 1975–87
ERIC/RCS

Introduction

Vocabulary knowledge is fundamental to reading comprehension; one cannot understand text without knowing what most of the words mean. A wealth of research has documented the strength of the relationship between vocabulary and comprehension. The proportion of difficult words in a text is the single most powerful predictor of text difficulty, and a reader's general vocabulary knowledge is the single best predictor of how well that reader can understand text (Anderson and Freebody 1981).

Increasing vocabulary knowledge is a basic part of the process of education, both as a means and as an end. Lack of adequate vocabulary knowledge is aleady an obvious and serious obstacle for many students, and their numbers can be expected to rise as an increasing proportion of them fall into categories considered educationally at risk. At the same time, advances in knowledge will create an ever larger pool of concepts and words that a person must master to be literate and employable.

The obviousness of the need and the strong relationship between vocabulary and comprehension invite a simplistic response: if we simply teach students more words, they will understand text better. However, not all vocabulary instruction increases reading comprehension. According to several studies, many widely used methods generally fail to increase comprehension (Mezynski 1983; Pearson and Gallagher 1983; Stahl and Fairbanks 1986).

Let me present the point in another way. Imagine an experiment with two groups of students about to read a selection from a textbook. One group is given typical instruction on the meanings of some difficult words from that selection; the other group receives no instruction. Both groups are then given the passage to read and are tested for comprehension. Do the students who received the vocabulary instruction do any better on the comprehension test? Very often they do not.

This news, if in fact it is news, should be unsettling. A major motivation for vocabulary instruction is to help students understand material they are about to read. If traditional instruction does not have this effect, teachers should know why not and what to do about it.

The purpose of this book is to lay out, on the basis of the best available research, how one can use vocabulary instruction most effectively to improve reading comprehension. The term *vocabulary* will be used primarily for *reading* vocabulary; the discussion will therefore be relevant primarily for students already past the initial stages of reading. For these students, learning new words means acquiring new meanings, not just learning to recognize in print words that are already a part of their oral vocabulary. Although the focus is on improving reading comprehension, some connections will be made to other aspects of instruction, linking vocabulary instruction and reading comprehension with broader goals of the language arts program.

Examples of useful approaches to vocabulary instruction — mainly, but not exclusively, prereading activities — will be presented for use or adaptation by classroom teachers. The primary purpose is not to provide a smorgasbord of activities, however. Rather, the purpose is to provide the teacher with a knowledge of how and why one can choose and adapt vocabulary-related activities to maximize their effectiveness.

Reasons for Failure of Vocabulary Instruction

Why does much vocabulary instruction often fail to increase comprehension measurably? There are two basic ways to account for this failure. The first is that most vocabulary instruction fails to produce in-depth word knowledge. A number of studies indicate that reading comprehension requires a high level of word knowledge — higher than the level achieved by many types of vocabulary instruction. Only those methods that go beyond providing partial knowledge, producing in-depth knowledge of the words taught, will reliably increase readers' comprehension of texts containing those words. The implication is that teachers should augment traditional methods of instruction such as memorizing definitions with more intensive instruction aimed at producing richer, deeper word knowledge.

A second reason for the failure of vocabulary instruction to improve reading comprehension measurably relates to the comprehensibility of texts containing some unfamiliar words. One does not need to know every word in a text to understand it. In one study, the researchers found that one content word in six could be replaced by a more difficult synonym without significantly decreasing comprehension (Freebody and Anderson 1983).

Hence, *redundancy of text* explains the failure of vocabulary instruction to improve comprehension. If a certain proportion of unfamiliar words in the text does not measurably hinder comprehension, then instruction on these words would not measurably improve it. In fact, inferring the meanings of unfamiliar words in text is itself a major avenue of vocabulary growth (Nagy, Anderson, and Herman 1987; Nagy, Herman, and Anderson 1985). By implication, what is needed to produce vocabulary growth is not more vocabulary instruction, but more reading.

These two accounts of the failure of some vocabulary instruction to improve comprehension appear to have almost contradictory implications for instruction. Yet the two are not mutually exclusive; they give complementary perspectives on the complex relationship between vocabulary knowledge and reading comprehension. After presenting each perspective and its instructional implications in detail, I will attempt to synthesize the two and recommend instruction that follows from this synthesis.

Partial Word Knowledge

The first reason given that vocabulary instruction often fails to produce measurable gains in reading comprehension is that much instruction does not produce a sufficient depth of word knowledge. There are degrees of word knowledge, ranging from "I think I've seen that word before" to "That's what I did my dissertation on." But what depth of word knowledge should teachers try to impart to their students? How well do readers have to know words to benefit from them in their reading?

This question can be answered in part by looking at studies that have tried to increase reading comprehension through vocabulary instruction. The level of word knowledge required for comprehension is shown by the types of vocabulary instruction that succeed or fail to produce gains in comprehension.

From the published research on vocabulary instruction, we can piece together a fairly consistent picture of the effectiveness of different types of instruction in increasing reading comprehension. In synthesizing this research, I will draw most heavily on McKeown et al. (1985), Mezynski (1983), Pearson and Gallagher (1983), and Stahl and Fairbanks (1986). Several valuable articles on this topic can also be found in the April 1986 *Journal of Reading*, a special issue devoted to vocabulary instruction.

Problems of Traditional Methods of Vocabulary Instruction

Much vocabulary instruction involves the use of definitions — some combination of looking them up, writing them down, and memorizing them. Another commonly used method involves inferring the meaning of a new word from the context. Neither method taken by itself, however, is an especially effective way to improve reading comprehension.

Definitional Approaches

Traditionally, much vocabulary instruction has involved some variety of a definitional approach: students learn definitions or synonyms for instructed words. There are obviously better and worse versions of this approach, and one should not conclude that definitions are not useful in vocabulary instruction. But definitions alone can lead to only a relatively superficial level of word knowledge. By itself, looking up words in a dictionary or memorizing definitions does not reliably improve reading comprehension.

The first problem with definitional methods of instruction is that many definitions simply are not very good. Here is a definition from a well-written school dictionary (*American Heritage School Dictionary* 1977):

> **mirror:** any surface that is capable of reflecting enough light without scattering it so that it shows an image of any object placed in front of it

This definition may be accurate, but it is hard to imagine that anyone who does not already know the meaning of the word could be helped by the definition. Most of the content words in the definition are less likely to be familiar to the student than the word *mirror* itself.

Here are some other definitions taken from the glossary of a basal reader:

> **siphon:** to pull water from one place to another
>
> **migration:** moving from one place to another
>
> **image:** likeness
>
> **baleen:** substance like horn that grows in plates in a whale's mouth and that is used to filter food from the water

These definitions are simply not accurate, at least not for the readers who need to use them. Note, for example, that *likeness* is relatively rare, occurring less than twice in a million words of text, whereas *image*, the word it is used to define, is far more frequent, occurring twenty-three times per million words of text (Carroll, Davies, and Richman 1971). *Likeness* is also one of the few English words ending in *-ness* that is semantically irregular. As for the definition of *baleen*, the words *horn* and *plates* may be frequent enough, but they are being used with meanings that are probably not at all familiar to students.

Definitions given in glossaries are also not always appropriate to the selection being read. In one basal reader, for example, *tragic* is defined in the glossary as "very sad." The word *tragic* occurs in one selection in the following context (spoken by a blind boy walking through Pompeii): "Too bad! The tragic poet is ill again. It must be a bad fever this time, for they're trying smoke fumes instead of medicine. I'm glad I'm not a tragic poet."

Even when definitions are accurate, they do not always contain enough information to allow a person to use the word correctly. This is especially true of definitions for words for concepts with which the learner is unfamiliar. Sheffelbine (1984) and others have used the following activity to communicate this point to teachers. Take some definitions of words that represent truly unfamiliar concepts — such as those in the list below — and try to do what students are often asked to do: "For each word, write a sentence in which it is used correctly." I suggest that readers actually take the time to try this activity, to experience the full force of the point: Definitions do not teach you how to *use* a new word. The definitions that follow appear in *Webster's Third New International Dictionary* (1961):

> **epiphenomenal:** having the character of or relating to an epiphenomenon
>
> **epiphenomenon:** a phenomenon that occurs with and seems to result from another
>
> **etaoin shrdlu:** a combination of letters set by running a finger down the first and then the second left-hand vertical banks of six keys of a linotype machine to produce a temporary marking slug not intended to appear in the final printing
>
> **kern:** to form or set (as a crop of fruit)
>
> **khalal:** of, relating to, or constituting the second of four recognized stages in the ripening of a date in which it reaches its full size and changes from green to red or yellow or a combination of the two colors
>
> **squinch:** a support (as an arch, lintel, or corbeling) carried across the corner of a room under a superimposed mass (as an octagonal spire or drum resting upon a square tower)
>
> **stative:** expressing a bodily or mental state
>
> **stirp:** the sum of the determinants of whatever nature in a fertilized egg

There are two reasons why it is difficult to write meaningful sentences, given only a definition. One is that definitions alone tell little about how a word is actually used. This problem is especially acute for children, who are less able than adults to use information that is available in definitions (Miller and Gildea 1987).

Another reason that it is difficult to write a sentence for a truly unfamiliar word, given only the definition, is that definitions do not effectively convey new concepts. One can think of it this way: Why isn't a glossary of biological terms an adequate substitute for a biology textbook? The answer in part is that important information about biological concepts and their interrelations simply does not fit into definitions.

This brings us to perhaps the most basic reason that knowledge of definitions is not adequate to guarantee comprehension of text containing the words defined: reading comprehension depends on a wealth of encyclopedic knowledge and not merely on definitional knowledge of the words in the text.

Take, for example, a narrative in which a bat is seen flying around. Definitional features of *bat* — the fact that bats are mammals rather than birds — may well be totally irrelevant in comprehending the text. Understanding the text may depend more on a knowledge of bats, or a knowledge of folklore about bats, that would not necessarily be included in a definition.

The point is not that definitions are never to be used in vocabulary instruction; on the contrary, they will play an essential role in most vocabulary instruction. But definitions as an instructional device have substantial weaknesses and limitations that must be recognized and corrected. How this can be done will become clearer from the discussion of intensive approaches to vocabulary instruction.

Contextual Approaches

Another common approach to teaching vocabulary is the use of context. A teacher might write a sentence or two containing the word to be learned on the board and ask students to figure out what the word means. There is no question that learning from context is an important avenue of vocabulary growth and that it deserves attention and practice in the classroom. But context, used as an instructional method by itself, is ineffective as a means of teaching new meanings, at least when compared with other forms of vocabulary instruction.

The problem is that, for the most part, a context may look quite helpful if one already knows what the word means, but it seldom supplies adequate information for the person who has no other knowledge about the meaning of a word. Consider the following sentence used to illustrate context clues involving contrast: "Although Mary was very thin, her sister was obese." Contrast is clearly involved, but the exact nature of the contrast is clear only to someone who already knows the meaning of *obese*. The problem becomes obvious when one attempts to substitute other words for the word whose meaning is supposed to be inferred. There is no reason, for example, for a word in this position to refer to an extreme value on the scale; an author could easily have used the word *normal* in this context. Given only this sentence context, one can think of other words that relate to other possible implicit contrasts — for example, *charitable* (in her description of Mary), or *unconcerned* (about her health). Nor is there any reason to restrict guesses about the meaning of a new word to synonyms; meanings can be expressed by phrases, such as "not jealous," that would fit in this context.

Note that this example involves the use of contrast, a relatively informative type of context clue. In most cases, what appears to be a fairly informative context would allow an even wider range of possible substitutions.

Natural and Instructional Contexts

One motivation for having students try to figure out word meanings from context is to help them develop word-learning strategies to use on their own. Practice in these strategies should definitely be part of an approach to vocabulary building. However, the teacher must face up to the dilemma posed by any attempt to teach such strategies: Most contexts in normal text are relatively uninformative. The context around any unfamiliar word tells us something about its meaning, but seldom does any single context give complete information (Deighton 1959; Shatz and Baldwin 1986). More informative contexts can be constructed (see Gipe 1979), but to the extent that they are informative, they are likely to be unnatural and hence defeat the purpose of training students in strategies for inferring word meanings from real texts.

A good context might help a student figure out the meaning of a less familiar synonym for a known word, but a single context is in general not adequate for teaching a new concept. If the goal is to teach students strategies, both teachers and students must accept partial word knowledge, some degree of uncertainty, and occasionally misleading contexts (Beck, McKeown, and McCaslin 1983). If the goal is to get a good grasp on the meaning of a new word, one will have to use highly artificial contexts, multiple contexts, or some other sort of supplemental information.

Combining Definitional and Contextual Approaches

A combination of definitional and contextual approaches is more effective than either approach in isolation; such mixed methods do, in general, increase reading comprehension (Stahl and Fairbanks 1986). Indeed, it would be hard to justify a contextual approach in which the teacher did not finally provide an adequate definition of the word or help the class arrive at one. Likewise, a good definitional approach includes sentences that illustrate the meaning and use of the words defined.

An example can often convey a meaning more vividly than a definition and help students relate what may be a very abstract and general definition to their own experience. For example, according to one school dictionary, the word *expand* in one sense means "to increase in one or more physical dimensions, as length or volume." A simple sentence such as "The balloon expanded as she blew air into it" might be helpful, perhaps even necessary, for the reader to make sense of such a general definition. It should be noted, of course, that it is the combination of definition and context that communicates the meaning effectively. The context alone, for example, "The balloon _____ as she blew it up," allows many interpretations: grew larger, burst, stretched, became taut, became more transparent, and so on.

Providing a natural context is often essential in teaching students how a word is used. Consider the definition of *cater*, meaning "to act with special consideration." Even if a student somehow grasped the connotations of this sense of the word (which the definition does not adequately convey), the student might produce a sentence such as "The mayor catered when the corporate executives visited the city."

Qualities of Effective Vocabulary Instruction

To be effective, then, vocabulary instruction must provide both adequate definitions and illustrations of how words are used in natural sounding contexts. But does supplying both definitions and contexts guarantee gains in reading comprehension? Not necessarily. It is safe to say that good definitions and contexts are minimal requirements for good instruction, but by no means do they exhaust what can be put into a good vocabulary lesson.

Methods of vocabulary instruction that most effectively improve comprehension of text containing the instructed words go far beyond providing definitions and contexts. Such methods can be referred to as "intensive vocabulary instruction." Numerous approaches to vocabulary fall under this heading. Rather than simply list them, I would like to try to identify some common properties or principles of effective vocabulary instruction. These principles should help teachers to generate and evaluate specific instructional techniques and also to adapt methods of vocabulary instruction effectively to particular classroom situations. Sample classroom activities consistent with the principles will be provided as a concrete help for the teacher.

A wide variety of additional vocabulary activities can be found in the April 1986 *Journal of Reading,* a special issue on vocabulary, or in Johnson and Pearson (1984).

Based on surveys of available research (see Stahl 1986; Graves and Prenn 1986; Carr and Wixson 1986), three properties of vocabulary instruction that is effective in increasing reading comprehension can be identified: integration, repetition, and meaningful use. Each of these will be discussed in turn.

Integration

The first property of powerful vocabulary instruction is that it integrates instructed words with other knowledge. This emphasis in instruction is an outgrowth of schema theory. For our purposes here, the essence of schema theory lies in two points: (1) that knowledge is structured — it consists not of lists of independent facts, but of sets of relationships, and (2) that we understand new information by relating it to what we already know.

Semantic Mapping

One classroom activity reflecting this emphasis has been called, among other things, "brainstorming" or "semantic mapping." This approach has been researched in some detail by Johnson and his colleagues (e.g., Johnson, Toms-Bronowski, and Pittelman 1982; see also Johnson and Pearson 1984). Many classroom applications of semantic maps (including those for vocabulary comprehension) are described in Heimlich and Pittelman (1986).

To focus on a vocabulary-related example, the teacher might choose one or more literary works related to a theme such as fear. (Or, given a particular story to be read, the teacher might identify a theme or topic central to that story.) In preparation, the teacher notes particular words in the selection relating to the theme, including but not necessarily limited to difficult words.

The first step in classroom instruction resembles Koch's (1980) language-generating games from *Wishes, Lies, and Dreams: Teaching Children to Write Poetry.* The teacher puts a word or phrase representing the basic theme on the board, then asks the students to write down individually any words they can think of related to this theme. Since the key word is *fear,* students will think of words such as *terror, ghosts, monsters, goose pimples,* and *scream.*

Next, the teacher makes a composite class list on the board, grouping — or having the students group — the words into categories when possible and helping the class agree on labels for the categories. The teacher can always prod students to think in new directions, for example, finding words about *not* being afraid — *brave, foolhardy,* and so forth. After the words have been categorized, the teacher can bring up any important words not suggested by the students and ask them to try to place them in an appropriate category. A semantic map resulting from the process might resemble the one in Figure 1.

The teacher can lead a discussion of how new words relate to familiar words and concepts and can ask students to relate stories about fears or frightening experiences that they or their friends or relatives have had. A rich vocabulary of words related to the theme of the selections to be studied has now been generated, and the students have related the theme to their own experiences.

In terms of language theory and research, this procedure serves several purposes. First of all, it activates appropriate background knowledge, getting students to think about experiences in their own lives that relate to the theme. This may seem unnecessary, but it has been found that students often do not spontaneously bring the knowledge they possess to bear when reading or when learning new words. Second, the procedure allows the teacher to identify and assess the specific background knowledge of the students in that class. The teacher can then make sure that new concepts and words are related to experiences that are meaningful to those particular students. Third, it provides a rich basis for further writing, as well as reading. Consistent with what Hillocks (1986) has called the "environmental approach," the teacher has given focus to student interaction while encouraging fluent and elaborated discussion. In summary, subsequent reading, talking, and writing are enriched by the brainstorming, mapping, and verbalizations of understandings and experiences in the prereading activities.

This approach to vocabulary instruction has some obvious limitations, however. Because it is designed for words that are related in some way, one cannot cover all of the words that might need some clarification in the selections to be read. (This is in fact a problem with many conceptually based approaches to vocabulary instruction.) It is best whenever possible to teach words in meaning-based groups, but this is not always easy for any given story. For example, in one teacher's manual the words listed for instruction for a story with the "fear" theme are *ominously, quaking, tarpaulin, serene, compose* (as in composure), *hedge, louvered, oblong, ebony,* and *forearms.* One cannot deal with all of these words in a single semantic mapping session and

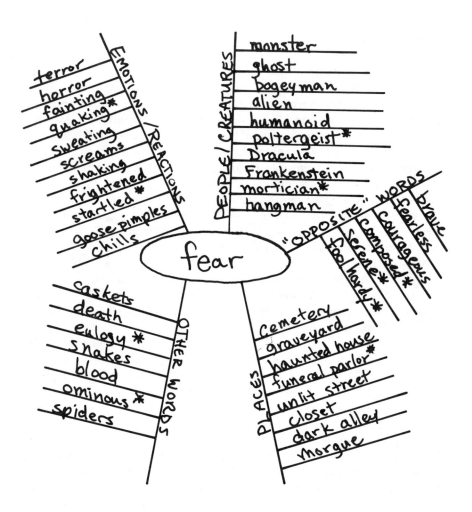

* Words introduced by the teacher

Figure 1. Semantic map (Little and Suhor 1987).

discussion. But one can pick a few words that relate to emotions, especially fear (*ominously, quaking, serene, compose*). In preparing for this lesson, the teacher may also find semantically related words to include in the instruction. Some might be found in the selection itself. In fact, the basal story for which the teacher's manual suggested *ominously, quaking, serene,* and *compose* for instruction also contained the words *courage, tremble, startle, awful, spooky, calm, shaking, excitement, terrified, amazed,* and *stunned.* Several of these words may be unfamiliar to some of the students.

There is no reason that students cannot be involved in spotting words and phrases related to a story's theme. An exercise by Little (1986), for example, makes students responsible for searching the first part of the text of O'Henry's "Gift of the Magi." As they do so, they get an initial sense of a theme of the story as well.

> Have your students list some words or phrases from the first five or six paragraphs that portray or give hints about Della and Jim's financial status. Then ask them to give a word or phrase that seems to them to describe accurately the financial condition of the young couple. (Some pertinent words and phrases in the text are "one dollar and eighty-seven cents"; "shabby little couch"; "mendicancy squad"; "shrunk to twenty dollars"; "saving every penny." Students will offer different words to accurately say how poor Della and Jim were. A few possibilities are *broke, penniless, impoverished, insolvent.*)

Of course, some stories might contain so few words related to any one theme or topic that any attempt to treat words in meaning-based groups may seem unprofitable. But there is no reason to organize vocabulary instruction strictly on the basis of the vocabulary found in the selection. Whenever possible, additional words that are related to the theme and are also generally useful should be included, as well as any words from a story on a related theme that is going to be read in the near future. The glossary of a textbook can often be used to find such words. For example, the glossary in the book containing the story about fear includes the words *amazement, appalled, anxiously, cringe, resolutely, sinister,* and *suspense.* It seems safe to assume that these words occur in other selections and that any time spent on them will not be wasted.

Semantic mapping may seem to blur the distinction between vocabulary instruction and other prereading activities aimed at helping students anticipate the general content or topic of the selection, activate relevant prior knowledge, and set a purpose for reading. One could argue that this blurring is actually a distinct advantage of semantic mapping. It can be tied in with other meaning-based approaches to prereading, such as discussion of personal experiences, role-playing activities, scenarios, case studies, and opinionnaires (Smagorinsky, McCann, and Kern 1987).

Semantic Feature Analysis

Effective vocabulary instruction integrates new information with familiar information; semantic mapping and similar techniques illustrate ways this can be done. Effective vocabulary instruction also should establish connections among the instructed items. Any instructional method such as semantic mapping that deals with words in groups based on related meanings or relationship to a common topic should help develop knowledge of relationships among the words being taught. However, some methods of instruction go beyond semantic mapping in the extent to which they focus on and specify such relationships. Semantic feature analysis is one of the instructional methods that deals most explicitly with relationships among word meanings. Johnson and Pearson (1984) describe the method in detail; see also Anders and Bos (1986) for a recent discussion.

Semantic feature analysis probably works best for words that form a semantically close-knit group. An example is the class of words including *house, mansion, shack, shed, barn, tent, bungalow,* and *shanty.* Some of the words should be familiar to the students already so that at least some of the distinctions in meaning are immediately understandable. These words are then used as labels for the rows in a two-dimensional matrix (Figure 2).

The vertical columns are for the "semantic features"; that is, phrases describing components of meaning shared by some of the words or that distinguish a word from other meanings. In the square representing the intersection of a given word and a given semantic feature, one records whether (or to what extent) this feature applies to this word. For example, a mansion is for people and is a permanent structure and therefore gets pluses in the corresponding columns. The features themselves, and the pluses and minuses in the matrix, are arrived at through class discussion. Depending on the words and features involved, it may be necessary to use question marks or zeros when specific features do not seem to apply to some of the words or when their value is not defined.

This activity can be open-ended. For example, to the words in Figure 2 one could add related words such as *garage, hangar, silo, manse, igloo,* or *hogan,* or perhaps even more distantly related words

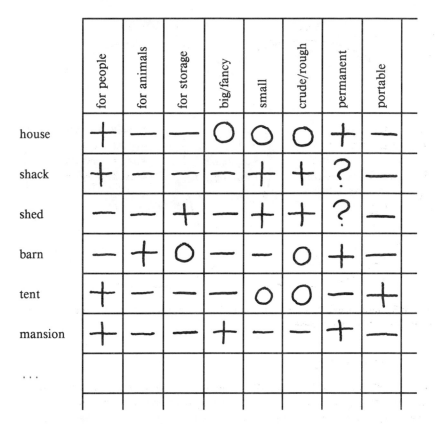

	for people	for animals	for storage	big/fancy	small	crude/rough	permanent	portable
house	+	—	—	O	O	O	+	—
shack	+	—	—	—	+	+	?	—
shed	—	—	+	—	+	+	?	—
barn	—	+	O	—	—	O	+	—
tent	+	—	—	—	O	O	—	+
mansion	+	—	—	+	—	—	+	—
. . .								

Figure 2. Matrix for a semantic feature analysis. The marks in the cells are arrived at through class discussion.

such as *hotel, skyscraper,* or *mall.* If such words are included, additional features must be found to discriminate among their meanings.

The Venn diagram is another device that applies semantic feature analysis in the classroom. In Figure 3 the basic concepts for comparison are *fable* and *fairy tale.* The terms and phrases describing what these concepts have in common are in the intersection of the two circles, while the features peculiar to only one of the literary forms are in the unconnected segments of each circle. Note that all terms might be key instructed words in genre study, and the diagram can be used either in prereading or as an integrating follow-up activity. Proett and Gill (1986) suggest broader uses of Venn diagrams, extending to character analysis in teaching the novel.

FABLE   FAIRY TALE

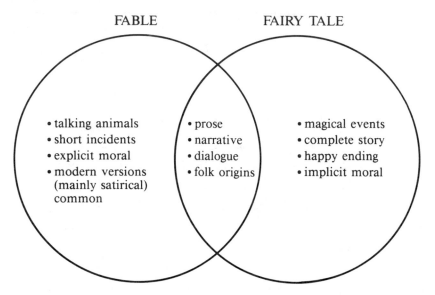

- talking animals   - prose   - magical events
- short incidents   - narrative   - complete story
- explicit moral   - dialogue   - happy ending
- modern versions   - folk origins   - implicit moral
  (mainly satirical)
  common

Figure 3. Venn diagram (Little and Suhor 1987). Elements within the intersection are common to both story types.

Hierarchical Arrays

Some meanings fall into hierarchical or taxonomic relationships. Names for organisms in biology are a prototypical example of this type of organization, but this type of structure can fit other types of meanings as well. Figure 4 illustrates how some of the meanings in Figure 2 might be fit into a hierarchical structure.

An interesting hierarchical structure for classroom use is presented in Kirby and Kuykendall's "Thinking Trees" (1985). This activity has the advantage of involving students in the generation of vocabulary items and in the explanation of meanings of words to each other — all within the context of an integrated language arts unit on the theme of "inventing" (Figure 5). Again, subsequent reading and writing are illuminated by the shared experiences of the students.

Linear Arrays

Linear arrays may be more appropriate for displaying other types of relationships among words. For example, many sets of words differ essentially in degree: *annoyed, angry, enraged,* and *furious;* or *lukewarm, warm, hot,* and *scalding.* The relationship among such words can be illustrated visually simply by arranging them in a line.

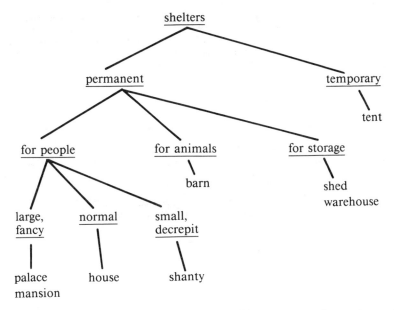

Figure 4. Hierarchical representation of relationships among word meanings, using meanings shown in Figure 2.

Students can be given the first two items in a sequence and asked to generate others, as in these examples:

sizable, large, . . . (huge, tremendous, immense)

whispering, talking, . . . (shouting, yelling, hollering, screaming)

ignore, allow, request, . . . (demand, insist, order)

Sequences such as these can be based on intensity, size, chronology, and position (New Orleans Public Schools 1972).

Whatever the particular structure used, comparing and contrasting related words is important for developing a greater sensitivity to meanings (Blachowitz 1986). For those sets of words that lend themselves to it, some sort of graphic representation of the relationships among meanings (such as those just discussed) may be helpful.

However, teachers can also help students explore relationships among words in less structured ways in classroom discussion. Fairly simple questions can prompt students to look for relationships among instructed words. Such questions constituted one part of the rich vocabulary instruction that Beck and her colleagues explored (Beck, McCaslin, and McKeown 1980; Beck, Perfetti, and McKeown 1982; Beck, McKeown, and Omanson 1987). In this program, the words

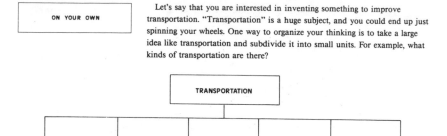

Let's say that you are interested in inventing something to improve transportation. "Transportation" is a huge subject, and you could end up just spinning your wheels. One way to organize your thinking is to take a large idea like transportation and subdivide it into small units. For example, what kinds of transportation are there?

Can you think of other kinds of transportation?

Now what kinds of problems are associated with cars? Can you think of other problems?

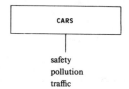

Now we're going to subdivide each problem associated with cars. Think about what kinds of solutions or inventions already exist to solve these problems. Make each problem the heading for a list. We've started the lists for you.

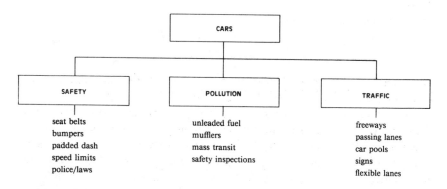

Can you list more in each category?

Figure 5. A "Thinking Tree" activity (Kirby and Kuykendall 1985). Working individually, students proceed from the broad topic, transportation, to specific problems associated with types of transportation. They then work together to develop other thinking trees.

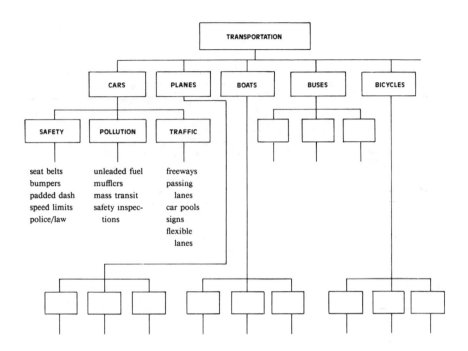

Can you think of anything not yet invented that might help solve the
problems of safety, pollution, and traffic? Make a list.

Figure 5 (continued). The above diagram has been slightly shortened for reprint in
this publication.

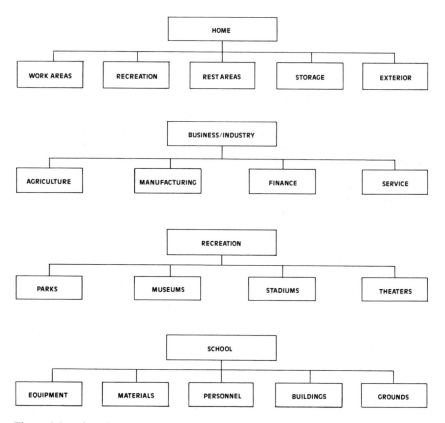

Figure 5 (continued)

being covered in any one week were all related to a common, broadly defined theme. With a set of words including *philanthropist, novice, virtuoso,* and *accomplice,* questions were posed about the relationships of these words: "Can a virtuoso be a novice?" "Is an accomplice likely to be a philanthropist?" "Can a virtuoso be a philanthropist?"

Emphasis on Concepts

The techniques above illustrate a number of ways that classroom instruction can integrate instructed words with other concepts and knowledge. However, more important than any specific techniques is the recognition that vocabulary instruction, at least once the students are past the initial stages of reading, must bring them to understand new concepts.

In the early stages of reading, a major goal is getting children to recognize in print words they already know and use orally. At this point, elaborate instruction on word meanings is often unnecessary, since the children already know the meanings. But by third or fourth grade, if not sooner, children will begin to see increasingly large numbers of words in print that they have never encountered before, either in print or in oral language.

Even when the teacher has begun to deal with words that are new to students, there is the danger of treating these new words simply as new labels, rather than as new concepts. Teachers can fall into the trap of thinking that hard words are only fancy ways of saying things that can be said with short, familiar words. Near synonyms seem to make such convenient definitions — *altercation* means *fight* or *argument; obese* means *fat; ancient* means *old; serene* means *calm.* Even vocabulary researchers sometimes wrongly assume that the meanings of new words can be adequately expressed in terms of a synonym or a brief phrase.

Synonyms and short definitions work well enough for some words, but relying on them too much reflects a rather dangerous oversimplification or misunderstanding of what learning vocabulary is about. Of course, one function of having a big vocabulary is to be able to impress people by using fancy words in place of simple ones. But teachers should be more interested in promoting new words as a way to enable students to conceive and express new ideas. The primary goal of vocabulary instruction, therefore, at least after the initial stages of reading, is not to teach students new labels, but to teach them new concepts.

One way that vocabulary instruction can be structured to ensure a focus on concepts rather than on labels is to start with instruction or discussion of the meaning of a word without mentioning the word itself. An example will make this clearer. The teacher might start discussing a word as follows: "Have you ever had the feeling that something was going to go wrong or that something bad was going to happen? Not that you had any good reason to think that — just a sort of a feeling. Has anyone ever had such a feeling? Did something bad actually happen?" The teacher might be able to extend the discussion for a minute or so before introducing the actual term: "Well, that sort of feeling is called a *premonition.*"

Discussing the concept before introducing the word may not always be the best way to teach new words; the teacher may often have good reasons for mentioning a word before discussing its meaning. But it is certainly a legitimate approach, one that forces the teacher and the class to treat new words as new concepts, and not just as new labels. Teaching concepts before labels may also help make vocabulary learning more interesting. Students are more likely to be motivated to remember the label for a concept they have begun to learn than to remember a new label in hopes that they will later find a use for it.

A discussion-based activity created by Little (1986) involves teaching a concept central to the study of several tenth grade literary selections about urban and rural life:

> Divide the class into two groups, assigning a recorder for each group. The groups will each be brainstorming word associations. One group should brainstorm as many words or phrases as they can connected with the word *city*. The other group should brainstorm words or phrases connected with the phrase *small town*. The recorder in each group should write down the words and phrases brainstormed.
>
> After giving the groups about three minutes for the brainstorming session, ask each recorder to read the group's list. Encourage students to ask questions about the words and allow them to express further ideas about the aptness of the words on their list. Then introduce the concept of *stereotype* to the students, explaining it in terms of oversimplified and formulaic views and attitudes about people, places, or institutions. Ask the students whether or not any of the items on their list reflected stereotypes of big cities or small towns and the people who live in them. Spend some time discussing stereotypes, noting that people and places do not often fit the stereotyped images used to describe them.

Another way to ensure that new words are dealt with as concepts and not just as labels is to consider examples and nonexamples and to discuss why the word applies or does not apply in each case. In the case of *premonition*, the teacher might consider a person who wakes up and remembers a dental appointment to get a tooth filled that day. The teacher can ask the class how that person might feel, whether that feeling could properly be termed a premonition, and why or why not. Well-chosen examples and nonexamples can illustrate important facets of the meaning of a new word. Students can also be asked to generate examples and nonexamples, which will tie in the new word with familiar concepts and experiences and also bring to light possible misunderstandings. (For more detailed discussions of teaching concepts through use of examples and nonexamples, see Klausmeier, Ghatala, and Frayer 1974; Markle 1975.)

Repetition

The first property of effective vocabulary instruction is integration — tying in new words with familiar concepts and experiences. The second property is *repetition*.

Repetition in word knowledge is related to what has been called the "verbal efficiency hypothesis" (Perfetti and Lesgold 1979), or the "bottleneck hypothesis." According to this hypothesis, a reader has only limited processing capacity available for tasks that require conscious attention. If the reader can decode well and knows all of the words in the text well, then identifying the words of the text can proceed more or less automatically so that most of the reader's attention can be given to comprehension.

Reading with understanding depends, then, on low-level processes such as decoding and word recognition proceeding smoothly without much conscious attention. Any interruption of the processes that are automatic for skilled readers can diminish comprehension. To take an extreme case, if a reader must struggle to decode the word *hippopotamus,* by the time that word has been recognized the reader may have forgotten what the rest of the sentence is about. Conversely, if this same reader is skillful in decoding, he or she can give more attention to the meaning of the sentence.

According to the verbal efficiency hypothesis, limited knowledge of word meanings can have the same sort of detrimental effect on comprehension that poor decoding skills may have. Being able to identify or produce a correct definition for a word does not guarantee that one will remember its meaning quickly and effortlessly during reading. Vocabulary instruction must therefore ensure not only that readers know what the word means, but also that they have had sufficient practice to make its meaning quickly and easily accessible during reading.

It should be stressed that repetition is necessary and worthwhile, at least for some words. According to available research, many encounters with a new word are necessary if vocabulary instruction is to have a measurable effect on reading comprehension (Stahl and Fairbanks 1986; McKeown et al. 1985).

How does a teacher provide multiple encounters with new words without having instruction become boring? The answer lies in the third property of effective vocabulary instruction, which I have labeled "meaningful use."

Meaningful Use

Effective vocabulary instruction helps the learner to use the instructed words meaningfully. One motivation for this property is simply that students learn more when they are actively involved. Another is what has been called "depth of processing." Simply stated, the more deeply some information is processed, the more likely it is to be remembered. In other words, vocabulary instruction that makes students think about the meaning of a word and demands that they do some meaningful processing of the word will be more effective than instruction that does not. A third motivation for instruction that requires learners to use the word meaningfully is, to put it simply, that you get what you train for. There is a big difference between being able to say what a word means and being able to use it. Knowing the definition of a word is often not enough to use the word properly. Conversely, we use and understand many words quite well without being able to define them. (How many educated adults can formulate a good, noncircular definition of *if?*)

If one's goal is to enable students to parrot definitions, drill on definitions is probably the most appropriate instructional technique. But if students are expected to deal with instructed words in context, the words must be encountered in context during instruction (McKeown et al. 1985). And if students are expected to learn to use words meaningfully in reading or writing, then instruction must include meaningful use of the words. Effective vocabulary instruction requires students to process words meaningfully — that is, make inferences based on their meanings — and includes tasks that are in some ways parallel to normal speaking, reading, and writing.

Instructional activities can elicit inferences through questions that require the student to use the meaning of the word to make an inference, rather than merely to state what the meaning is. Compare the two types of multiple choice questions below. The first type asks the student to identify the meaning of *gendarme;* the second asks the student to use the meaning to make an inference. In this example, the difference between the two types of items has been made minimal to focus on the essence of the difference:

1. Identifying the meaning of a word
   Gendarme means: a. bellboy
                         b. policeman
                         c. waiter
                         d. letter carrier

2. Using the meaning of a word
   A gendarme is most likely to carry: a. a suitcase
                                          b. a gun
                                          c. a tray
                                          d. the mail

In practice, of course, it would be even better to use a format that is much closer to the normal use of words in reading, for example, by presenting the target word in a complete sentence, followed by a question that requires using the meaning to make a more extended inference. This point is illustrated well by one of the methods of assessing in-depth word knowledge that McKeown et al. (1985) used. In a sample item from their "context interpretation task," the student is given the sentence, "When father heard that Lisa had ripped up the letter from Steve, father commended her for it." The student is then asked, "What do you think father thought of Steve?"

A classroom activity called "Frequent Contact" (Jantzen 1985) involves discussion of inferences about clusters of related words. A graphic array is involved, and the activity leads to a writing assignment in which students' extensions of words in the "Teenager" list mentioned below are a partial basis for the narrative:

> Draw three columns on a sheet of paper, with the headings Soldiers, Guitarists, and Teenagers. Place the words from the list that follows in the appropriate column, based on whether a soldier, a guitarist, or a teenager would be most likely to have the *most frequent* contact with each item. Use the dictionary if you aren't sure of the meaning of a word. If a word has several meanings and could appear in more than one column, consider all of the applicable meanings, and remember the instructions: place the word according to the likelihood of *most frequent* contact by a soldier, guitarist, or teenager.

amplifier	cafeteria	dog	LP
billets	carbine	dogtag	major
bicycle	chords	drill	PX
bluejeans	computer	fatigues	pick
bridge	desk	frets	staff

> After you have completed your categorizations, draw a circle around those words that have more than one meaning and caused you to consider putting them in more than one column.
>
> Have a volunteer draw three columns on the board and enter his or her categorizations. Discuss differences between your list and the one on the board and explain the reasons for your categorizations. In some cases, an equally strong argument might be made for placing a word in two different categories. Do not

argue about whose answer is "right" in such cases. The important thing is to make the reasons for your choice clear to others.

Compare your circled words with those of your classmates. Explain why you decided to categorize those words as you did. (pp. 104–5)

The intensive program of instruction outlined by Beck, McCaslin, and McKeown (1980) includes a number of activities that require students to use, and not just to state, the meanings of instructed words. In a word-association activity, the teacher says a familiar word, and the students are supposed to respond with a closely related word selected from among those being taught. Suppose the day's words are *virtuoso, philanthropist, accomplice,* and *novice,* and the teacher says "crook." Students would be expected to respond with the word *accomplice* and to be able to defend their choice.

Another activity is completion of sentences containing, for example, the target words "The accomplice was worried because _____ ." The use of sentence completion, as opposed to the more open-ended task of "using this word in a sentence," helps steer students in the direction of sentences that really use the meaning of the word, instead of producing stereotyped answers of the form "I saw an X yesterday."

The exact nature of the task is not the issue, and any of these or similar tasks can be adapted for particular classrooms and particular types of words. What is important is that students be given practice at tasks that require them to use, rather than simply to state, the meanings of words they are learning. These tasks should include at least some in which the instructed words are embedded in natural sentence contexts.

The goal of meaningful use is combined with brainstorming, visual arrays of words, inferring, gathering opinions, and discussing in the AIM Game (Suhor 1983). Classroom teachers have used this integrative prereading technique in grades seven through twelve and as a prereading activity in literature and reading textbooks:

> The AIM Game is a pre-reading sequence in three parts, geared towards involving students in activities that will make their reading a short story more interesting — and more perceptive. . . .
> The teacher pre-selects an appropriate theme and one or more stories that deal with the theme. In the example below, the theme is the relationship between human beings and modern technology. Possible short stories include Donald Barthelme's "Report," Ray Bradbury's "The Rocket Man," Frank Brown's "Singing Dinah's Song," Robert F. Young's "Thirty Days Had September," and Kurt Vonnegut's "Epicac." (There are dozens of other stories, of course, on the humanity/technology theme.)

As the game progresses, students create their own vocabulary list of words related to the theme, explore relationships among words on the vocabulary list, and exchange opinions with regard to the theme. The AIM Game — which usually takes from two to four class periods — has three steps:

1. **Associating Ideas** — A brainstorming activity in which students in small groups play two word-association games using words related to the theme.

2. **Ideas that Match** — A relationship-making exercise in which students, using the two word lists generated in Step 1, make up five pairs of words by matching words from their first word-association list with words from their second word-association list.

3. **My Opinion, Your Opinion** — A discussion game in which students explain why they agree or disagree with five "Opinion Statements" related to the theme.

Associating Ideas. Divide your class into groups of four or five students. Ask each group to appoint a recorder who will write down the words called out by other group members. Then give the groups ninety seconds to brainstorm as many words as possible associated with the word "computer." When time is up, the recorder for each group counts and reads aloud the words generated by the group. Have students repeat the process above, using a different sheet of paper to list words that they associate with the word "freedom."

Ideas that Match. Have the students in each group match up five words from their "computer" list with five words from their "freedom" list. Unlike the brainstorming game, this step is untimed, and the students should be able to explain in their own words *how* each of the five word-pairs is justified. For example, the students in a group might match the word *document* from their "computer" list with the word *Constitution* from their "freedom" list. They should be able to support the matchup, if called upon to do so, with a statement like "The U.S. Constitution is a kind of document" — a categorization relationship according to specific example/general type.

A member of each group should write the five word pairs on the chalkboard so other groups can read them and ask for an explanation of the relationships that aren't obvious. The nature of the matchup can be any kind of relationship — synonymity, anonymity, categorization, cause-effect, analogy, etc. — that can be explained informally by the students in a group.

My Opinion, Your Opinion. Write the following Opinion Statements on the chalkboard, or give students dittoed copies of the statements. Ask them to read silently and decide, on an individual basis, whether they *agree* or *disagree* with each statement.

Circle the "A" if you agree with the statement. Circle the "D" if you disagree.

A D 1. The world of the future will be a better place for humanity.

A D 2. With computers and machines playing such a big part in our lives, we have a tendency to lose contact with nature.

A D 3. Humanity can dream great dreams, but they aren't likely to come true.

A D 4. Someday computers and machines will free us from hard labor.

A D 5. Computers and machines could become so important in our lives that they would actually rule us.

Discuss each statement with the class, asking initially how many agreed and how many disagreed. Don't try to arrive at a "right" answer, but encourage the students to explain *why* they felt as they did, exchanging ideas freely on each of the statements. Often, students will change their opinions during the course of the discussion as the statements are examined closely and the students explore their feelings more fully.

The students are now ready to read Barthelme's "Report," or a similar story on the theme of humans and technology. Note that in Step 1, the students created their own vocabulary list of words associated with themes in the unit. (Teachers report that words on the students' lists often appear in the short story, in fact.) In Step 2, the students' thinking skills were challenged as they put together (often humorously or ingeniously) pairs of words associated with the theme. In Step 3, they clarified their own ideas on crucial issues that the author raises in the story. The students themselves, in a sense, are "authors" of words and ideas on how human beings relate to technology. They are prepared to experience Barthelme's exploration of the theme.

Efficiency of Vocabulary Instruction

Up to now, we have been considering only one of the reasons that some vocabulary instruction fails to improve reading comprehension. Much of the available research indicates that fairly intensive vocabulary instruction is needed to guarantee measurable gains because readers must possess in-depth knowledge of a substantial proportion of the words in a text before comprehension can proceed smoothly.

At this point, one might draw the conclusion that effective vocabulary instruction for comprehension would require the teachers to devote absurdly large amounts of time and energy to vocabulary instruction. They would have to cover every word in the selection that students might not know with rich, intensive instruction that ties the words in with background knowledge, engaging the students actively in meaningful processing, and would have to do all of this ten or more times per word (see McKeown et al. 1985). This conclusion presents the teacher with a dilemma: there does not appear to be enough time to bring students to the level of word knowledge that seems to be necessary for comprehending texts.

Fortunately, this bleak conclusion is based on a consideration of only one of the reasons that vocabulary instruction often fails to increase reading comprehension.

Redundancy of Text

The arguments for intensive instruction are based on the fact that many types of vocabulary instruction have been found not to increase reading comprehension. Comprehension of text often requires much richer knowledge of a word than simple definitional knowledge. Another consideration, however, is the redundancy of text — the fact that readers can tolerate a certain proportion of unknown words in text without comprehension being disrupted.

If a certain amount of unknown words does not decrease comprehension measurably, it stands to reason that teaching students the meaning of those words is not going to increase comprehension either. And if students can understand a text without any knowledge of some of the words, it follows that teachers need not give intensive instruction on all of the words in the text.

How many unknown words can students tolerate in text? Freebody and Anderson (1983) found that replacing one content word in six with a difficult synonym did not reliably decrease sixth graders' comprehension of text. In other words, readers may be able to tolerate texts in which as many as 15 percent of the words are not fully known. The comprehensibility of cloze passages with one-word-in-five or one-word-in-ten deletion patterns leads to a similar conclusion. The proportion of unfamiliar words that a reader normally encounters is likely to be lower. Reanalysis of data reported by Anderson and Freebody (1983) indicates that, for the average fifth grader, about 3 percent of the words in school texts would not be known at even a lenient criterion of word knowledge, and about 6 percent would not be known if a more stringent criterion were adopted.

Exactly what proportion of unknown words readers can tolerate depends on the nature of the text, the role of the unfamiliar words in the text, and the purpose for reading. In any case, students do not have to know *all* of the words in a text to read it with a high level of comprehension. The teacher need not set the unrealistic goal of giving intensive instruction on every unfamiliar word in a text.

Incidental Word Learning

Another reason that intensive instruction is unnecessary for every unfamiliar word in a text is that reading itself is a major avenue for learning the meanings of unfamiliar words.

Very few people indeed have been subjected to systematic, intensive, and prolonged vocabulary instruction of the sort that would guarantee gains in reading comprehension. Yet many people have managed to acquire extensive reading vocabularies. Few vocabulary programs, no matter how ambitious, cover more than several hundred words in the course of a year. And yet recent research indicates that school children's vocabularies grow at the rate of 3,000 new words annually (Miller and Gildea 1987; Nagy and Herman 1987).

People learn words from a number of sources — from the speech of parents and peers, from classroom lectures and discussion, from television, and of course from *reading*. After third grade, for those children who do read a reasonable amount, reading may be the single largest source of vocabulary growth. Fielding, Wilson, and Anderson (1986) found that the amount of free reading was the best predictor of vocabulary growth between grades two and five.

There may appear to be a contradiction at this point. I argued earlier that context is a relatively ineffective method of vocabulary instruction and that most contexts in natural texts are relatively uninformative, if not misleading. How can one of the less effective means of vocabulary learning be the single largest source of vocabulary growth?

The answer appears to lie in sheer volume. In a recent study, Nagy, Anderson, and Herman (1987) measured incidental learning from context by students in the third, fifth, and seventh grades. They found that students who read grade-level texts under fairly natural conditions had about a one-in-twenty chance of learning the meaning of any particular word from context. At first glance, this finding only confirms that learning from context is an ineffective method. And as far as short-term instructional strategies are concerned, this is true.

However, the short term is not the whole picture. We estimate that the average fifth grader spends about twenty-five minutes a day reading, when reading both in and out of school is taken into account. Given this amount of reading, we estimate that a student will encounter about 20,000 unfamiliar words a year. If one in twenty of these is learned from context, this would amount to a gain of about a thousand words per year, or a third of the average child's annual vocabulary growth. If teachers could add another twenty-five minutes per day to a child's reading time, an additional thousand words could be learned each year. If high quality texts appropriate for the child were chosen, this rate of learning could be more than doubled.

But what about the quality of word knowledge gained from context? To improve reading comprehension, children need rich, in-depth knowledge of words. What about the three properties essential to powerful vocabulary instruction — integration, repetition, and meaningful use? Does learning from context supply these?

A single encounter with a word in context obviously does not. This is why context is not especially effective as a method of instruction. But regular, extensive reading can supply all of the characteristics of powerful vocabulary instruction.

Consider the first property, integration — the need to relate the meaning of a new word to the students' prior knowledge. If the reader is largely successful in comprehending the text containing the new word, then the new word *is* being tied in with the reader's prior knowledge; most of the words and the concepts in the text are already at least partly familiar. As for repetition, whether reading supplies this for a new word depends on how much the student is reading and whether the new word is repeated. If the most important words for a student to learn are those that do occur repeatedly, reading will supply the necessary repetition. And of course in reading, one makes meaningful use of words. Reading is the best practice for reading.

Given that many people do develop in-depth knowledge of large numbers of words apart from much vocabulary instruction, wide reading must be able to produce the kind of word knowledge necessary for reading comprehension. Furthermore, given the number of words to be learned and the number of encounters it takes to learn them thoroughly, reading is necessarily the major avenue of large-scale vocabulary growth.

The Trade-off between Effective Instruction and Incidental Learning

So far, two seemingly contradictory conclusions have been drawn from the failure of some vocabulary instruction to improve reading comprehension. On the one hand, comprehension of text depends on knowledge much richer than simply knowing the definitions of words. In at least some cases, then, vocabulary instruction must be rich enough to really teach students new concepts. This must be done in a way that helps them relate new information to what they already know and provides them with enough practice so that they can quickly and flexibly apply their knowledge of the instructed words in real reading. An extreme response to this point might be to devote the bulk of the school day to intensive vocabulary instruction. On the other hand, comprehension of text does not require in-depth knowledge of every word in the text. Rather, reading itself is the major avenue of acquiring in-depth knowledge of words. An extreme response to this point would be to abandon vocabulary instruction altogether.

The contradiction is of course only apparent. The resolution lies in the teacher's ability to make efficient use of vocabulary instruction — to identify the words and concepts that are likely to pose serious difficulties for the students, the type of difficulties, and the most appropriate instructional remedies.

If students are to achieve both the depth and breadth of vocabulary knowledge that they will need to become proficient adult readers, they must have many encounters with large numbers of words — encounters that help them relate the word to their own prior knowledge and experiences and that give them practice in using their growing knowledge of these words to make inferences. The experiences with words that lead to large-scale vocabulary growth come through both explicit instruction and incidental encounters with words in reading. A division of labor between instruction and incidental learning is clearly necessary.

Most growth in vocabulary knowledge must necessarily come through reading. There is no way that vocabulary instruction alone can provide students with enough experiences with enough words to produce both the depth and breadth of vocabulary knowledge that they need to attain. Increasing the volume of students' reading is the single most important thing a teacher can do to promote large-scale vocabulary growth.

On the other hand, some vocabulary instruction is necessary. In some cases, context never seems to provide the crucial information; each of us can probably think of a dozen or so words we have encountered frequently while reading without having gained any real understanding of their meaning. And in some cases, comprehension of a text depends crucially on knowledge of specific words that may not be familiar to some students.

The teacher's goal must therefore be to find the optimal division of labor between incidental learning and explicit vocabulary instruction — to know how much time and energy to spend on teaching word meanings and how much to depend on the students' ability to learn on their own.

The best balance depends on the particular students, texts, and words involved. It would be foolish to formulate any hard-and-fast rules here. But some principles can help a teacher know how to get the best returns on time and energy devoted to vocabulary instruction. The key issue is to identify the specific type of difficulties posed by different words in the text and to adapt instruction to deal efficiently with them. More specifically, one needs to choose words very carefully for intensive instruction and make strategic use of minimal instruction.

Choice of Words for Intensive Instruction

Intensive vocabulary instruction is needed to produce word knowledge of any depth. However, only a fraction of the potentially unfamiliar words in a story can be covered by such instruction, so one must decide when it is really called for. What sort of words in a selection require this kind of attention?

Intensive instruction is most appropriate, first of all, for words that are conceptually difficult, those representing complex concepts that are not part of students' everyday experience. Second, such instruction usually depends on having a group of words that have related meanings (or that at least all relate to a single topic). Third, intensive instruction is most worthwhile when the words to be covered are important, in either of two senses: important to the understanding of a selection or important because of their general utility in the language. Intensive instruction is also called for if one wants students to incorporate the instructed words into their writing or speaking vocabularies (Duin and Graves 1987).

There is only one criterion I did not mention that might be expected to be first on the list — one might think that intensive instruction is most necessary for those words that are least familiar to the students. It is true that the students' familiarity with the words should play some role in the teacher's selection, but familiarity cannot be the primary criterion.

On the one hand, the words in a selection that are least familiar to the class may not be especially suited for intensive instruction — for example, they may be peripheral to the story and not conceptually complex. Conversely, some conceptually difficult words that are important to the selection may be superficially familiar to the students. Even if the students can quote a definition for such words, it does not necessarily follow that they know them well enough to comprehend the passage. Time might be better spent on words that are already partially known, if a deeper knowledge of them is necessary for understanding the text, than on less familiar words not crucial to the story.

For the teacher who is trying to determine when intensive instruction is most necessary, the single most important question is which words are conceptually difficult for the reader. Jenkins and Dixon (1983), Graves and Prenn (1986), and others have made it clear that it is essential to recognize different types of vocabulary-learning situations for different words. Students already have some words in their oral vocabularies, and they only have to learn to decode them. Other words represent new labels for familiar concepts, and still others represent new concepts that must be learned. Traditional vocabulary instruction using only definitions or context is unlikely to enable students to learn concepts that are really new to them; it is in this case that intensive instruction is most needed.

When is a word conceptually difficult? *Superfluous* sounds like a hard word. It is long. But the concept it represents probably is not all that novel to many students. They may already know the word *unnecessary*. An example or so may be quite enough to tie the word *superfluous* in with experiences and concepts familiar to students.

Superconductor is difficult in a different sense. To understand it, one needs some grasp of several concepts relating to electricity, resistance, and so on. *Superconductor* is part of a whole system of technical concepts that would probably be unfamiliar to most students.

Can adults' judgments of the conceptual difficulty of a word tell us anything about how difficult the students actually find these words? Nagy, Anderson, and Herman (1987) looked at the extent to which different properties of words influenced the probability that the meanings of these words would be learned from context during normal reading. Among several word properties considered was a rating of conceptual difficulty performed by two of the authors, one an experienced teacher. It was found that only rated conceptual difficulty influenced learning from context. Words at the highest level of conceptual difficulty were not learned during one reading of a text, even in expository texts that had as an explicit purpose teaching these very concepts. In fact, in texts with a high proportion of conceptually difficult words (including many expository texts and materials containing terms from a particular discipline or profession), relatively little incidental learning of new word meanings occurred.

Difficult concepts can be acquired incidentally from text, but how well depends heavily on the quality of the text. Herman et al. (1987)

were able to produce a substantial increase in the amount of incidental word learning by making expository texts more conceptually explicit; that is, by clearly stating the relationships among concepts and the relationships of new concepts to familiar ones in the text.

However, many texts read in school involve large numbers of technical terms and are not conceptually explicit. Definitions alone will not convey new concepts adequately. Intensive vocabulary instruction is especially useful when new and difficult concepts are under study. And while all aspects of intensive instruction are important for such concepts, integration — that is, tying the new concept in with familiar concepts and experience and making the relationships among concepts clear — should be a major goal.

The conceptual difficulty of the whole text, and not just the conceptual difficulty of individual words, must be taken into account in determining when intensive vocabulary instruction is needed. A comparison of studies on the effects that vocabulary instruction has on comprehension suggests that the greater the proportion of unfamiliar words in the text, the more intensive the instruction required to improve comprehension.

An informal and enjoyable student search for meanings of multiple technical terms is modeled in a prereading exercise by Little and Suhor (1987). Based on an excerpt from *Byrd Lives,* Ross Russell's biography of the jazz great Charlie Parker, the exercise includes terms that provide a schema for understanding the world of the musicians:

> The main background that students will need for reading this biographical excerpt is the vocabulary related to music, especially jazz. Not every technical term in the selection needs to be known, but some of the more important and interesting ones can be handled in a prereading assignment that makes use of the students themselves, other teachers in your school, and students' friends and relatives as resources.

1. rhythm section	10. bridge
2. high-hat cymbal	11. changes
3. territorial band	12. chords
4. casuals	13. modulations
5. jam session	14. embouchure
6. improvise	15. vibrato
7. ideas	16. perfect pitch
8. riff	17. cabaret
9. boogie-woogie	18. speakeasy

At least two days before the students read "Charlie Parker —

A Kansas City Jam Session," place the above words on the chalkboard. Explain that the words appear in a selection they will read soon, a biography about a jazz musician. Ask if anyone in the class can explain, in his or her own words, the meanings of any of the terms. Point out that some of the words, such as "ideas" and "changes," have a special meaning in the world of jazz. (Note: Six of the eighteen items — numbers 6, 7, 9, 11, 12, and 13 — will be conceptually difficult for nonmusical students.)

For words not adequately defined in the class session, ask for volunteers to seek out further informal definitions from music students they know, music teachers in your school, and friends or relatives who play music. Stress that clear informal definitions and explanations are being sought, not standard dictionary-like definitions. Plain-language explanations might even be clearer than technical dictionary definitions. In fact, the first twelve terms are used mainly by jazz and popular music artists, so dictionary definitions might not be available.

Strategic Use of Minimal Instruction

Intensive vocabulary instruction may be called for in the case of some words. But what does one do with the rest of them? The most important question to ask may be: What words will I not have to teach at all? If one can find words that are not crucial to getting the gist of the story, it is not absolutely necessary to teach them. There is only so much time, and ultimately time spent in reading is what should be maximized. If some of the unfamiliar words in a selection occur in reasonably informative contexts, it may be profitable to save them for a postreading activity in which students try to infer their meanings from the surrounding text.

Efficient use of vocabulary instruction also depends on distinguishing the types of difficulties that different words pose for readers. For some words, the primary problem may be decoding, rather than meaning; brief attention to the pronunciation of the word might be adequate in such cases.

As a general principle, it is valuable to have students hear or use a word in natural sentence contexts. But even this principle has exceptions; I would rather have students spend a few seconds looking at a picture of an armadillo than have them practice using the word *armadillo* in a sentence. Conversely, for words with derivational suffixes, such as *argument* or *decision,* an example of how the word is used in a sentence may convey the meaning more quickly than either a picture or a definition can.

Then there may be some words for which a definition is adequate. Teachers should remain profoundly distrustful of definitions, for reasons already discussed. However, if a word is peripheral to the theme of the selection being read and is not conceptually complex, and if an available definition is accurate and explains the meaning in terms of words and concepts familiar to the reader, learning the definition may give the student a good start at learning the word.

Those conditions are often fulfilled in the study of literature, especially in word play and in the reading of poetry. For example, teachers often help students to define the words *suffice, cranny, essayed,* and *lamentable* in the context of studying the lines in the poems below.

In Frost's "Fire and Ice":

> I think I know enough of hate
> To say that for destruction ice
> Is also great
> And would suffice.

In Tennyson's "Flower in the Crannied Wall":

> Flower in the crannied wall,
> I pluck you out of the crannies, . . .

In Stephen Crane's "There Was a Man":

> Who essayed to sing,
> And in truth it was lamentable.

Similar ad hoc opportunities for initial learning of words frequently occur in connection with puns and other language play and in the study of science fiction. In-depth knowledge of the word will of course come only with many meaningful encounters, and these will come with regular reading.

If children are to learn large numbers of words, they need to be exposed to them. Teachers should include as rich a vocabulary as they can in their own speech without losing the students. The classroom can be made into a vocabulary-rich environment in numerous and varied ways without making vocabulary a chore.

Promoting Independent Word Learning

There are more words to be learned than can be covered in even the most ambitious program of vocabulary instruction, and there is more to be learned about each word than can be covered in even the most intensive instruction. To promote large-scale, long-term vocabulary growth, teachers must aim at increasing students' incidental word learning.

Students must be given as much opportunity as possible for incidental word learning. This means increased time spent actually reading. I want to stress that the single most important thing a teacher can do to promote vocabulary growth is to increase students' volume of reading. Increasing out-of-school reading is important, but one must also be careful that preparation for reading (including vocabulary instruction) does not steal too much time from reading itself. Also keep in mind that any activity which increases reading comprehension, if coupled with the opportunity to read, will result in vocabulary growth.

But students can be helped in specific ways as well to become better independent word learners so that they benefit more from whatever reading they do. Unfortunately, it is beyond the scope of this book to treat this topic in the depth it deserves. One problem is that research documenting which methods of instruction actually increase independent word learning has simply not yet been done. I will, however, briefly suggest some ways that independent word learning can be increased.

Two widely used methods of helping students learn to deal with unfamiliar words on their own are context and structural analysis. There is no doubt that skilled word learners use context and their knowledge of prefixes, roots, and suffixes to deal effectively with new words. I see two primary ways that instruction in both of these areas can be made more effective. First of all, the teacher should take care to teach these methods as strategies, modelling for students how knowledge of context and word parts can help the reader deal with unfamiliar words encountered while reading and giving them ample opportunity for guided practice in these strategies with realistic examples. Although learning word meanings from context is a "natural" way to learn vocabulary, it cannot be assumed that younger or less able students are proficient at it (see McKeown 1985).

Second, teachers should be aware, and make their students aware, of the limitations of these methods. Contexts often give only partial, if not misleading, clues to the meaning of a new word. Contrary to the impression one gets from some advocates of structural analysis, knowing that *abs* means "away from" and *tract* means "to draw, pull" is not likely to help a student encountering the word *abstract* for the first time.

Much more research is necessary to determine how best to teach the use of context clues and word structure analysis. But in the meantime, teachers can do much to help students become better word learners. Most of all, recognizing that explicit vocabulary instruction can cover only a fraction of the words students need to learn can help teachers approach vocabulary instruction in ways that will increase independent learning.

The use of dictionaries is one example. Having students look up definitions is not especially effective at producing in-depth word knowledge; besides, students find it rather boring. On the other hand, ability to use a dictionary is an important skill, and looking through dictionaries can be fascinating. Knowing this, a teacher can minimize copying definitions and similar activities that might lead to a lifelong dislike for learning words, and instead maximize activities treating dictionary use as a skill to be mastered.

Realizing that only a fraction of the words students must learn can be covered also changes the way a teacher might evaluate the cost of more intensive vocabulary instruction. Only if one feels free from the obligation to teach about every potentially unfamiliar word in a selection is there enough time to treat any of the words in depth. Even then, more intensive vocabulary instruction appears relatively expensive, both in terms of preparation time and classroom time. But more intensive instruction, if done well, is also far more interesting than memorizing definitions. For example, low-income urban fourth graders, after five months of the intensive vocabulary instruction implemented by Beck and her colleagues (Beck, McCaslin, and McKeown 1980), were disappointed when the program was over and asked for more. During the program, students participated actively and both noticed and used the instructed words outside the vocabulary lessons. There may well be substantial long-term gains in vocabulary growth from the higher levels of interest and motivation produced by intensive instruction.

Conclusion

The purpose of this book has been not to present specific new techniques of vocabulary instruction, but to describe how different approaches to vocabulary contribute to reading comprehension. It is hoped that this information will provide teachers with a basis for using and effectively adapting different instructional techniques, as well as with the motivation to sometimes use methods of instruction that appear to have a greater initial cost.

References

The American Heritage School Dictionary. 1977. Boston: Houghton Mifflin.

Anders, P., and C. Bos. 1986. Semantic Feature Analysis: An Interactive Strategy for Vocabulary Development and Text Comprehension. *Journal of Reading* 29: 610–16.

Anderson, R. C., and P. Freebody. 1981. Vocabulary Knowledge. In *Comprehension and Teaching: Research Reviews,* ed. J. Guthrie, 77–117. Newark, Del.: International Reading Association.

———. 1983. Reading Comprehension and the Assessment and Acquisition of Word Knowledge. In *Advances in Reading/Language Research,* ed. B. Hutson, 231–56. Greenwich, Conn.: JAI Press.

Beck, I., M. McCaslin, and M. McKeown. 1980. *The Rationale and Design of a Program to Teach Vocabulary to Fourth-Grade Students.* Pittsburgh: University of Pittsburgh, Learning Research and Development Center.

Beck, I., M. McKeown, and E. McCaslin. 1983. All Contexts Are Not Created Equal. *Elementary School Journal* 83: 177–81.

Beck, I., M. McKeown, and R. Omanson. 1987. The Effects and Uses of Diverse Vocabulary Instructional Techniques. In *The Nature of Vocabulary Acquisition,* ed. M. McKeown and M. Curtis. Hillsdale, N.J.: Erlbaum.

Beck, I., C. Perfetti, and M. McKeown. 1982. The Effects of Long-Term Vocabulary Instruction on Lexical Access and Reading Comprehension. *Journal of Educational Psychology* 74: 506–21.

Blachowitz, C. 1986. Making Connections: Alternatives to the Vocabulary Notebook. *Journal of Reading* 29: 643–49.

Carey, S. 1978. The Child as Word Learner. In *Linguistic Theory and Psychological Reality,* ed. M. Halle, J. Bresnan, and G. Miller. Cambridge, Mass.: MIT Press.

Carr, E., and K. Wixson. 1986. Guidelines for Evaluating Vocabulary Instruction. *Journal of Reading* 29: 588–95.

Carroll, J. B., P. Davies, and B. Richman. 1971. *Word Frequency Book.* New York: American Heritage.

Clark, E. V. 1973. What's in a Word? On the Child's Acquisition of Semantics in His First Language. In *Cognitive Development and the Acquisition of Language,* ed. T. E. Moore. New York: Academic Press.

Deighton, D. 1959. *Vocabulary Development in the Classroom.* New York: Bureau of Publications, Teachers College, Columbia University.

Duin, A., and M. Graves. 1987. Intensive Vocabulary Instruction as a Prewriting Technique. *Reading Research Quarterly* 22: 311–30.

Fielding, L. G., P. T. Wilson, and R. C. Anderson. 1986. A New Focus on Free Reading: The Role of Trade Books in Reading Instruction. In *The Contexts of School-Based Literacy,* ed. T. Raphael. New York: Random House.

Freebody, P., and R. C. Anderson. 1983. Effects on Text Comprehension of Different Proportions and Locations of Difficult Vocabulary. *Journal of Reading Behavior* 15: 19–39.

Gipe, J. 1979. Investigating Techniques for Teaching Word Meanings. *Reading Research Quarterly* 14: 624–44.

Graves, M., and M. Prenn. 1986. Costs and Benefits of Various Methods of Teaching Vocabulary. *Journal of Reading* 29: 596–602.

Heimlich, J., and S. Pittelman. 1986. *Semantic Mapping: Classroom Applications.* Newark, Del.: International Reading Association.

Herman, P. A., R. C. Anderson, P. D. Pearson, and W. Nagy. 1987. Incidental Acquisition of Word Meanings from Expositions with Varied Text Features. *Reading Research Quarterly* 22: 263–84.

Hillocks, G., Jr. 1986. *Research on Written Composition.* Urbana, Ill.: National Conference on Research in English and the ERIC Clearinghouse on Reading and Communication Skills.

Jantzen, S. 1985. *Scholastic Composition. Level 2.* New York: Scholastic Inc.

Jenkins, J., and R. Dixon. 1983. Vocabulary Learning. *Contemporary Educational Psychology* 8: 237–60.

Johnson, D., and P. D. Pearson. 1984. *Teaching Reading Vocabulary* (2d Ed.) New York: Holt, Rinehart & Winston.

Johnson, D., S. Toms-Bronowski, and S. Pittelman. 1982. *An Investigation of the Effectiveness of Semantic Mapping and Semantic Feature Analysis with Intermediate Grade Level Children* (Program Report 83–3). Madison: Wisconsin Center for Educational Research, University of Wisconsin.

Kirby, D., and C. Kuykendall. 1985. *Thinking through Language, Book One.* Urbana, Ill.: National Council of Teachers of English.

Klausmeier, H. J., E. S. Ghatala, and D. A. Frayer. 1974. *Conceptual Learning and Development: A Cognitive View.* New York: Academic Press.

Koch, K., and The Students of P.S. 61 in New York City. 1980. *Wishes, Lies, and Dreams: Teaching Children to Write Poetry.* New York: Harper and Row.

Little, D. 1986. Pre-Reading and Post-Reading Activities for Tenth Graders. Unpublished manuscript.

Little, D., and C. Suhor. 1987. Pre-Reading — Jargon and Shop Talk. Unpublished manuscript.

Markle, S. M. 1975. They Teach Concepts, Don't They? *Educational Researcher* 4: 3–9.

McKeown, M. 1985. The Acquisition of Word Meaning from Context by Children of High and Low Ability. *Reading Research Quarterly* 20: 482–96.

McKeown, M., I. Beck, R. Omanson, and M. Pople. 1985. Some Effects of the Nature and Frequency of Vocabulary Instruction on the Knowledge and Use of Words. *Reading Research Quarterly* 20: 222–35.

Mezynski, K. 1983. Issues Concerning the Acquisition of Knowledge: Effects of Vocabulary Training on Reading Comprehension. *Review of Educational Research* 53: 253–79.

Miller, G., and P. Gildea. 1987. How Children Learn Words. *Scientific American* 257(3): 94–99.

Nagy, W., R. C. Anderson, and P. Herman. 1987. Learning Word Meanings from Context during Normal Reading. *American Educational Research Journal* 24: 237–70.

Nagy, W., and P. Herman. 1987. Breadth and Depth of Vocabulary Knowledge: Implications for Acquisition and Instruction. In *The Nature of Vocabulary Acquisition*, ed. M. McKeown and M. Curtis. Hillsdale, N.J.: Erlbaum.

Nagy, W., P. Herman, and R. C. Anderson. 1985. Learning Words from Context. *Reading Research Quarterly* 20: 233–53.

New Orleans Public Schools. 1972. *Guidelines for the English Program in the Middle School and the Junior High School.* Division of Instruction, New Orleans Public Schools.

Pearson, P. D., and M. Gallagher. 1983. The Instruction of Reading Comprehension. *Contemporary Educational Psychology* 8: 317–44.

Perfetti, C., and A. Lesgold. 1979. Coding and Comprehension in Skilled Reading and Implications for Reading Instruction. In *Theory and Practice of Early Reading* (Vol. 1), ed. L. B. Resnick and P. Weaver. Hillsdale, N.J.: Erlbaum.

Proett, J., and K. Gill. 1986. *The Writing Process in Action: A Handbook for Teachers.* Urbana, Ill.: National Council of Teachers of English.

Sanders, G. D., J. H. Nelson, and M. L. Rosenthal, eds. 1970. *Chief Modern Poets of Britain and America.* London, England: The Macmillan Co.

Schatz, E. K., and R. S. Baldwin. 1986. Context Clues Are Unreliable Predictors of Word Meanings. *Reading Research Quarterly* 21: 429–53.

Sheffelbine, J. L. 1984. *Teachers' Decisions about the Utility of Dictionary Tasks and the Role of Prior Knowledge.* Paper presented at the annual meeting of the National Reading Conference, St. Petersburg, Fla.

Smagorinsky, P., T. McCann, and S. Kern. 1987. *Explorations: Introductory Activities for Literature and Composition.* Urbana, Ill.: National Council of Teachers of English.

Stahl, S. 1986. Three Principles of Effective Vocabulary Instruction. *Journal of Reading* 29: 662–68.

Stahl, S., and M. Fairbanks. 1986. The Effects of Vocabulary Instruction: A Model-Based Meta-Analysis. *Review of Educational Research* 56: 72–110.

Suhor, C. 1983. The AIM Game: A Pre-Reading Strategy for Teaching Short Story. *Illinois English Bulletin* 70, no. 3: 1–3.

Webster's Third New International Dictionary of the English Language, Unabridged. 1961. Springfield, Mass.: G. & C. Merriam.

Author

William Nagy is a senior scientist at the Center for the Study of Reading, University of Illinois at Urbana-Champaign. His research on vocabulary acquisition and vocabulary instruction has been published in *Reading Research Quarterly, American Educational Research Journal,* and Center for the Study of Reading Technical Reports.